Pebble® Plus

Baby Animals

T0052997

A Baby Duck Story

by Martha E. H. Rustad

Consulting Editor: Gail Saunders-Smith, PhD

Consultant: Marsha A. Sovada, PhD, Research Wildlife Biologist
Northern Prairie Wildlife Research Center
U.S. Geological Survey, Jamestown, North Dakota

CAPSTONE PRESS
a capstone imprint

A mother duck sits and sits.

Her eggs stay warm in her nest.

Crack! Crack!

That egg has a tiny hole.

Now another, and another!

One by one, tiny ducklings

push out using an egg tooth.

Brr! They're wet and cold.

But duckling feathers dry

and fluff up quickly.

Let's go!

Mother duck waddles

from her nest.

Follow in a line.

Keep up! Don't get lost.

Jump right in. Splash!

Paddle around the pond.

Move those webbed feet

to swim.

Hop out, and shake off

that water.

Cuddle close to mom.

Oil from her feathers

rubs off on us.

Quack, quack, cheep!

I'm hungry.

How about you?

Grab food with your bill.

Watch out!

That fox just tried to eat you.

Mom hissed and quacked

and chased it off.

She keeps us safe.

Let's play and chase.

We're growing bigger
every day.

Pick and preen.

Fluffy feathers fall out.

Sleek feathers grow in.

Use your bill to spread

oil over them.

Today's the day!

I'll fledge and fly.

Good-bye, mom. Good-bye,

brothers and sisters.

I'm on my own.

Glossary

bill—the hard, pointed part of a bird's mouth

egg tooth—a toothlike part that sticks out on a duckling's bill; the egg tooth falls off after the duck hatches

fledge—to grow feathers big enough for flying; ducklings fledge at about two months of age

preen—to clean and arrange feathers with a bill; ducks spread oil from a gland near their tail on their feathers when they preen; oil keeps their feathers waterproof

sleek—smooth and shiny

waddle—to walk with short steps while moving from side to side

webbed—having folded skin or tissue between an animal's toes or fingers; ducks use their webbed feet to swim

Read More

Johnson, Jinny. *Duck*. How Does It Grow? Mankato, Minn.: Smart Apple Media, 2010.

Savage, Stephen. *Duck*. Animal Neighbors. New York: PowerKids Press, 2009.

Steinkraus, Kyla. *Ducks on the Farm*. Farm Animals. Vero Beach, Fla.: Rourke Pub., 2011.

Internet Sites

FactHound offers a safe, fun way to find Internet sites related to this book. All of the sites on FactHound have been researched by our staff.

Here's all you do:

Visit *www.facthound.com*

Type in this code: 9781429660655

Super-cool stuff! Check out projects, games and lots more at **www.capstonekids.com**

Pebble Plus is published by Capstone Press,
1710 Roe Crest Drive, North Mankato, Minnesota 56003.
www.capstonepub.com

Library of Congress Cataloging-in-Publication Data
Rustad, Martha E. H. (Martha Elizabeth Hillman), 1975–
  A baby duck story / by Martha E. H. Rustad.
    p. cm.—(Pebble plus. Baby animals)
  Includes bibliographical references and index.
  ISBN 978-1-4296-6065-5 (library binding)
  ISBN 978-1-4296-7091-3 (paperback)
  1. Ducklings—Juvenile literature. I. Title. II. Series.
  QL696.A52R86 2012
  598.4'1139—dc22   2010053921

Summary: Full-color photographs and simple text describe how ducklings grow up.

Editorial Credits
Erika L. Shores, editor; Ashlee Suker, designer; Svetlana Zhurkin, media researcher;
    Laura Manthe, production specialist

Photo Credits
Dreamstime/400ex127, 20–21; Fedotishe, 9; Ina Van Hateren, 19; Kwiktor, 1, 16–17; Zepherwind, cover
iStockphoto/Melissa Carroll, 4–5; rotofrank, 3
Photolibrary/Daniel Cox, 15
Shutterstock/Iliuta Goean, 12–13; Jan de Wild, 7; pfalztv, 11

The author dedicates this book to her son Markus Johan Rustad.

Note to Parents and Teachers

The Baby Animals series supports national science standards related to life science.
This book describes and illustrates ducklings. The images support early readers in
understanding the text. The repetition of words and phrases helps early readers learn
new words. This book also introduces early readers to subject-specific vocabulary words,
which are defined in the Glossary section. Early readers may need assistance to read
some words and to use the Glossary, Read More, Internet Sites, and Index sections of
the book.

Printed in the United States   4798

Index

Word Count: 178
Grade: 1
Early-Intervention Level: 17